POPE FRANCIS
IN THE U.S.

POPE FRANCIS IN THE U.S.

WORDS OF MERCY AND HOPE

Introduced and compiled
by Marianne Lorraine Trouvé, FSP

BOOKS & MEDIA

Boston

Library of Congress Control Number: 2015955023

Excerpts from Pope Francis' Masses, meetings, visits, vigils, vespers and encyclicals copyright © Libreria Editrice Vaticana. All rights reserved. Used with permission.

Cover design by Rosana Usselmann

Cover photo by © Jeffrey Bruno / ALETEIA

Interior graphic elements designed by Freepick.com

Published by Pauline Books & Media, 50 Saint Paul's Avenue, Boston, MA 02130–3491

Printed in the U.S.A.

www.pauline.org

Pauline Books & Media is the publishing house of the Daughters of St. Paul, an international congregation of women religious serving the Church with the communications media.

1 2 3 4 5 6 7 8 9   19 18 17 16 15

Contents

List of Abbreviations

BCR   Holy Mass with Bishops, Clergy, and Religious of Pennsylvania, *Cathedral of Saints Peter and Paul, Philadelphia, Saturday, September 26, 2015*

CFC   Visit to Detainees at Curran-Fromhold Correctional Facility, *Philadelphia, Sunday, September 27, 2015*

GOV   Greeting to the Organizers, Volunteers, and Benefactors of the World Meeting of Families, *Philadelphia International Airport, Sunday, September 27, 2015*

GZM   Interreligious Meeting, *Ground Zero Memorial, New York, Friday, September 25, 2015*

Introduction

POPE FRANCIS came to America with a message of faith, mercy, and hope. From September 22 to 27, 2015, he visited Washington, D.C.; New York City; and Philadelphia. Francis was the first pope to address a joint session of Congress. He also spoke at the United Nations and shared his concerns with leaders from all over the world.

What are his concerns? He brought up the causes that are especially close to his heart, such as respect for human life in all stages; serving the poor and immigrants; the importance of the family, peace, religious freedom, mission, and Christian witness; and care for the earth as our home. He knew how to adapt his message to the varied audiences he addressed—from Congress to the homeless, from the U.N. to inmates at a Philadelphia prison, from bishops to school children.

The purpose of this volume is to present the message of Pope Francis in a way best adapted to individual readers. It does not focus so much on the bigger issues of policy for the nation and the world, but how we as Christians can make the Gospel fruitful in our lives today. Excerpts were selected from his various addresses with a view to his personal appeal to each one of us and arranged by themes. Pope Francis often speaks in a very simple way, a way that most people can easily relate to. He's not asking us to do anything extraordinary, but simply to fully live the commitment of our Baptism. If each one of us did that, the Church and the world would be radically changed for the good.

God at Our Side

THE HEART of the Pope expands to include everyone. To testify to the immensity of God's love is the heart of the mission entrusted to the Successor of Peter, the Vicar of the One who on the cross embraced the whole of mankind. May no member of Christ's Body or the American people feel excluded from the Pope's embrace. Wherever the name of Jesus is spoken, may the Pope's voice also be heard to affirm that: *"He is the Savior!"*

MBW

TO THIS end, it is important that the Church in the United States also be a humble home, a family fire that attracts men and women through the attractive light and warmth of love.

MBW

MAY THE forthcoming Holy Year of Mercy, by drawing us into the fathomless depths of God's heart in which no division dwells, be for all of you a privileged moment for strengthening communion, perfecting unity, reconciling differences, forgiving one another, and healing every rift, that your light may shine forth like *"a city built on a hill"* (Mt 5:14).

MBW

WE NEED to learn from Jesus, or better [yet] to learn Jesus, meek and humble; to enter into his meekness and his humility by contemplating his way of acting.

MBW

REJOICE IN the Lord always! I say it again, rejoice! . . . Something deep within us invites us to rejoice and tells us not to settle for placebos that always keep us comfortable.

JSW

WE ALL know the struggles of everyday life. So much seems to stand in the way of this invitation to rejoice. Our daily routine can often lead us to a kind of glum apathy that gradually becomes a habit, with a fatal consequence: our hearts grow numb.

JSW

WE DON'T want apathy to guide our lives . . . or do we? We don't want the force of habit to rule our lives . . . or do we? So we ought to ask ourselves: What can we do to keep our hearts from growing numb, becoming anesthetized? How do we make the joy of the Gospel increase and take deeper root in our lives?

JSW

JOSEPH WAS someone who asked questions. But first and foremost, he was a man of faith. Faith gave Joseph the power to find light just at the moment when everything seemed dark. Faith sustained him amid the troubles of life. Thanks to faith, Joseph was able to press forward when everything seemed to be holding him back.

SPW

FAITH MAKES us know that God is at our side, that God is in our midst, and his presence spurs us to charity. Charity is born of the call of a God who continues to knock on our door, the door of all people, to invite us to love, to compassion, to service of one another.

SPW

JESUS KEEPS knocking on our doors, the doors of our lives. He doesn't do this by magic, with special effects, with flashing lights and fireworks. Jesus keeps knocking on our doors in the faces of our brothers and sisters, in the faces of our neighbors, in the faces of those at our side.

SPW

DEAR FRIENDS, one of the most effective ways we have to help is that of prayer. Prayer unites us; it makes us brothers and sisters. It opens our hearts and reminds us of a beautiful truth we sometimes forget. In prayer, we all learn to say "Father," "Dad." And when we say "Father," "Dad," we learn to see one another as brothers and sisters. In prayer, there are no rich or poor; there are sons and daughters, sisters and brothers. In prayer, there is no first or second class; there is brotherhood.

SPW

IN PRAYER, our hearts find the strength not to be cold and insensitive in the face of situations of injustice. In prayer, God keeps calling us, opening our hearts to charity.

SPW

HOW GOOD it is for us to pray together.

SPW

JOY SPRINGS from a grateful heart. Truly, we have received much, so many graces, so many blessings, and we rejoice in this. It will do us good to think back on our lives with the grace of remembrance.

VPR

A GRATEFUL heart is spontaneously impelled to serve the Lord and to find expression in a life of commitment to our work. Once we come to realize how much God has given us, a life of self-sacrifice, of working for him and for others, becomes a privileged way of responding to his great love.

VPR

YET, IF we are honest, we know how easily this spirit of generous self-sacrifice can be dampened.

VPR

THE TRUE worth of our apostolate is measured by the value it has in God's eyes. To see and evaluate things from God's perspective calls for constant conversion . . . it calls for great humility. The cross shows us a different way of measuring success. Ours is to plant the seeds; God sees to the fruits of our labors. And if at times our efforts and works seem to fail and produce no fruit, we need to remember that we are followers of Jesus . . . and his life, humanly speaking, ended in failure, in the failure of the cross.

VPR

THE OTHER danger comes when we become jealous of our free time, when we think that surrounding ourselves with worldly comforts will help us serve better. The problem with this reasoning is that it can blunt the power of God's daily call to conversion, to encounter with him.

Slowly but surely, it diminishes our spirit of sacrifice, our spirit of renunciation and hard work.

VPR

DEAR BROTHERS and sisters, shortly, in a few minutes, we will sing the Magnificat. Let us commend to Our Lady the work we have been entrusted to do; let us join her in thanking God for the great things he has done, and for the great things he will continue to do in us and in those whom we have the privilege to serve. Amen.

VPR

THE PROPHET Isaiah can guide us in this process of "learning to see." He speaks of the light that is Jesus. And now he presents Jesus to us as "Wonderful Counselor, the Mighty God, the Everlasting Father, the Prince of Peace." In this way, he introduces us to the life of the Son, so that his life can be our life.

MSG

NO ONE or anything can separate us from his love. Go out and proclaim, go out and show that God is in your midst as a merciful Father who himself goes out, morning and evening, to see if his son has returned home and, as soon as he sees him coming, runs out to embrace him. This is beautiful. An embrace that wants to take up, purify, and elevate the dignity of his children. A Father who, in his embrace, is "glad tidings to the poor, healing to the afflicted, liberty to captives, comfort to those who mourn" (Is 61:1–2).

MSG

DEAR BROTHERS and sisters, I thank you for the way in which each of you has answered Jesus' question, which inspired your own vocation: "What about you?" I encourage you to be renewed in the joy and wonder of that first encounter with Jesus, and to draw from that joy renewed fidelity and strength.

BCR

WITH GRATITUDE for all we have received, and with confident assurance in all our needs, we turn to Mary, our Blessed Mother. With a mother's love, may she intercede for the growth of the Church in America in prophetic witness to the power of her Son's cross to bring joy, hope, and strength into our world. I pray for each of you, and I ask you, please, to pray for me.

BCR

JESUS WAS not a confirmed bachelor, far from it! He took the Church as his bride and made her a people of his own. He laid down his life for those he loved, so that his bride, the Church, could always know that he is God with us, his people, his family. We cannot understand Christ without his Church, just as we cannot understand the

Church without her spouse, Christ Jesus, who gave his life out of love, and who makes us see that it is worth the price.

PVF

I DARE say that at the root of so many contemporary situations is a kind of impoverishment born of a widespread and radical sense of loneliness. Running after the latest fad, accumulating "friends" on one of the social networks, we get caught up in what contemporary society has to offer: Loneliness with fear of commitment in a limitless effort to feel recognized.

MBP

I AM here as a pastor, but above all as a brother, to share your situation and to make it my own. I have come so that we can pray together and offer our God everything that causes us pain, but also everything that gives us hope, so that we can receive from him the power of the resurrection.

CFC

WE ALL know that life is a journey, along different roads, different paths, which leave their marks on us.

CFC

WE ALSO know in faith that Jesus seeks us out. He wants to heal our wounds, to soothe our feet that hurt from traveling alone, to wash each of us clean of the dust from our journey. He doesn't ask us where we have been; he doesn't question us about what we have done. Rather, he tells us: "Unless I wash your feet, you have no share with me" (Jn 13:8). Unless I wash your feet, I will not be able to give you the life that the Father always dreamed of, the life for which he created you. Jesus comes to meet us so that he can restore our dignity as children of God. He wants to help us to set out again, to resume our journey, to recover our hope, to restore our faith and trust. He wants us to keep walking along the paths of life, to realize that we have a mission, and that confinement is never the same thing as exclusion.

CFC

LIFE MEANS "getting our feet dirty" from the dust-filled roads of life and history. All of us need to be cleansed, to be washed. All of us. Myself, first and foremost. All of us are being sought out by the Teacher, who wants to help us resume our journey. The Lord goes in search of us; to all of us he stretches out a helping hand.

CFC

ALL OF us have something we need to be cleansed of, or purified from. All of us. May the knowledge of this fact inspire us all to live in solidarity, to support one another and seek the best for others.

CFC

LET US look to Jesus, who washes our feet. He is "the way, and the truth, and the life." He comes to save us from the lie that says no one can change, the lie of thinking that no one can change. Jesus helps us to journey along the paths of life and fulfillment. May the power of his love and his resurrection always be a path leading you to new life.

CFC

OUR FATHER will not be outdone in generosity and he continues to scatter seeds. He scatters the seeds of his presence in our world, for "love consists in this, not that we have loved God but that *he loved us*" first (I Jn 4:10). That love gives us the profound certainty that we are sought by God; he waits for us. It is this confidence that makes disciples encourage, support, and nurture the good things happening all around them. God wants all his children to take part in the feast of the Gospel. Jesus says, "Do not hold back anything that is good; instead, help it to grow!" To raise doubts about the working of the Spirit, to give the impression that it cannot take place in those who are not "part of our group," who are not "like us," is a dangerous temptation. Not only does it block conversion to the faith; it is a perversion of faith!

MWM

FAITH OPENS a "window" to the presence and working of the Spirit. It shows us that, like happiness, holiness is always tied to little gestures. "Whoever gives you a cup of water in my name will not go unrewarded," Jesus says (see Mk 9:41). These little gestures are those we learn at home, in the family; they get lost amid all the other things we do, yet they do make each day different. They are the quiet things done by mothers and grandmothers, by fathers and grandfathers, by children, by brothers and sisters. They are little signs of tenderness, affection, and compassion. Like the warm supper we look forward to at night, the early meal awaiting someone who gets up early to go to work. Homely gestures. Like a blessing before we go to bed, or a hug after we return from a hard day's work. Love is shown by little things, by attention to small daily signs that make us feel at home. Faith grows when it is lived and shaped by love. That is why our families, our homes, are true domestic churches. They are the right place for faith to become life and life to grow in faith.

MWM

JESUS TELLS us not to hold back these little miracles. Instead, he wants us to encourage them, to spread them. He asks us to go through life, our everyday life, encouraging all these little signs of love as signs of his own living and active presence in our world.

MWM

POINTEDLY, YET affectionately, Jesus tells us: "If you, who are evil, know how to give good gifts to your children, how much more will the heavenly Father give the Holy Spirit to those who ask him!" (Lk 11:13). How much wisdom there is in these few words! It is true that, as far as goodness and purity of heart are concerned, we human beings don't have much to show! But Jesus knows that, where children are concerned, we are capable of boundless generosity. So he reassures us: if only we have faith, the Father will give us his Spirit.

MWM

MAY GOD grant that all of us may be prophets of the joy of the Gospel, the Gospel of the family and family love, as disciples of the Lord. May he grant us the grace to be worthy of that purity of heart that is not scandalized by the Gospel! Amen.

MWM

WE KNOW with certainty that evil never has the last word, and that, in God's merciful plan, love and peace triumph over all.

GOV

Do Unto Others

WHENEVER A hand reaches out to do good or to show the love of Christ, to dry a tear or bring comfort to the lonely, to show the way to one who is lost or to console a broken heart, to help the fallen or to teach those thirsting for truth, to forgive or to offer a new start in God . . . know that the Pope is at your side, the Pope supports you. He puts his hand—a hand wrinkled with age, but by God's grace still able to support and encourage—in your own.

MBW

OURS MUST not be just any kind of prayer, but familiar union with Christ, in which we daily encounter his gaze and sense that he is asking us the question: *"Who is my mother? Who are my brothers?"* (Mk 3:31–34). One in which we can calmly reply: *"Lord, here is your mother, here are your brothers! I hand them over to you; they are the ones whom you entrusted to me."*

MBW

WHEN THE stranger in our midst appeals to us, we must not repeat the sins and the errors of the past. We must resolve now to live as nobly and as justly as possible, as we educate new generations not to turn their backs on our "neighbors" and everything around us. Building a nation calls us to recognize that we must constantly relate to others, rejecting a mindset of hostility in order to adopt one of reciprocal subsidiarity, in a constant effort to do our best. I am confident that we can do this.

USC

ON THIS continent, too, thousands of persons are led to travel north in search of a better life for themselves and for their loved ones, in search of greater opportunities. Is this not what we want for our own children? We must not be taken aback by their numbers, but rather view them as persons, seeing their faces and listening to their stories, trying to respond as best we can to their situation. To respond in a way that is always humane, just, and fraternal. We need to avoid a common temptation nowadays: to discard whatever proves troublesome. Let us remember the Golden Rule: "Do unto others as you would have them do unto you" (Mt 7:12).

USC

THIS [GOLDEN] Rule points us in a clear direction. Let us treat others with the same passion and compassion with which we want to be treated. Let us seek for others the same possibilities we seek for ourselves. Let us help others to grow, as we would like to be helped ourselves. In a word, if we want security, let us give security; if we want life, let us give life; if we want opportunities, let us provide opportunities. The yardstick we use for others will be the yardstick that time will use for us. The Golden Rule also reminds us of our responsibility to protect and defend human life at every stage of its development.

USC

I WOULD encourage you to keep in mind all those people around us who are trapped in a cycle of poverty. They too need to be given hope. The fight against poverty and hunger must be fought constantly and on many fronts, especially in its causes. I know that many Americans today, as in the past, are working to deal with this problem.

USC

THE BIBLE is very clear about this: there was no room for them. I can imagine Joseph, with his wife about to have a child, with no shelter, no home, no place to stay. The Son of God came into this world as a homeless person. The Son of God knew what it was to start life without a roof over his head. We can imagine what Joseph must have been thinking. How is it that the Son of God has no home? Why are we homeless? Why don't we have housing? These are questions that many of you may ask, and do ask, every day. Like Saint Joseph, you may ask: Why are we homeless, without a place to live? And those of us who do have a home, a roof over our heads, would also do well to ask: Why do these, our brothers and sisters, have no place to live? Why are these brothers and sisters of ours homeless?

SPW

REST IS needed, as are moments of leisure and self-enrichment, but we need to learn how to rest in a way that deepens our desire to serve with generosity. Closeness to the poor, the refugee, the immigrant, the sick, the exploited, the elderly living alone, prisoners, and all God's other poor, will teach us a different way of resting, one that is more Christian and generous.

VPR

TO ENABLE these real men and women to escape from extreme poverty, we must allow them to be dignified agents of their own destiny. Integral human development and the full exercise of human dignity cannot be imposed. They must be built up and allowed to unfold for each individual, for every family, in communion with others, and in a right relationship with all those areas in which human social life develops— friends, communities, towns and cities, schools, businesses and unions, provinces, nations, etc. This presupposes and requires the right to education—also for girls (who are excluded in certain places)—which is ensured first and foremost by respecting and reinforcing the primary right of the family to educate its children, as well as the right of churches and social groups to support and assist families in the education of their children.

UNO

IN BIG cities, beneath the roar of traffic, beneath "the rapid pace of change," so many faces pass by unnoticed because they have no "right" to be there, no right to be part of the city. They are the foreigners, the children who go without schooling, those deprived of medical insurance, the homeless, the forgotten elderly. These people stand at the edges of our great avenues, in our streets, in deafening anonymity. They become part of an urban landscape that is more and more taken for granted in our eyes, and especially in our hearts.

MSG

AMONG US today are members of America's large Hispanic population, as well as representatives of recent immigrants to the United States. Many of you have emigrated (I greet you warmly!) to this country at great personal cost, in the hope of building a new life. Do not be discouraged by whatever hardships you face. I ask you not to forget that, like those who came here before you, you bring many gifts to this nation. Please, you should never be ashamed of your traditions. Do not forget the lessons you learned from your elders, which are something you can bring to enrich the life of this American land. I repeat, do not be ashamed of what is part of you, your life blood. You are also called to be responsible citizens, and to contribute fruitfully—as those who came before you did with such fortitude—to the life of the communities in which you live. I think in particular of the vibrant faith so many of you possess, the deep sense of family life, and all those other values that you have inherited. By contributing your gifts, you will not only find your place here, you will help to renew society from within. Do not forget what took place here over two centuries ago. Do not forget that Declaration that proclaimed that all men and women are created equal, that they are endowed by their Creator with certain inalienable rights, and that governments exist in order to protect and defend those rights.

IMP

JESUS SAYS in the Scriptures: "Truly, I say to you, as you did it to one of the least of these my brethren, you did it to me." Your care for me and your generous welcome are a sign of your love for Jesus and your faithfulness to him. So, too, is your care for the poor, the sick, the homeless, and the immigrant, your defense of life at every stage, and your concern for family life. In all of this, you recognize that Jesus is in your midst and that your care for one another is care for Jesus himself.

GOV

A NATION can be considered great when it defends liberty as Lincoln did; when it fosters a culture that enables people to "dream" of full rights for all their brothers and sisters, as Martin Luther King [Jr.] sought to do; when it strives for justice and the cause of the oppressed, as Dorothy Day did with her tireless work; [when it nurtures]

the fruit of a faith that becomes dialogue and
sows peace in the contemplative style of Thomas
Merton.

God's Gift
of the Family

IN JESUS, God himself became Emmanuel, God-with-us, the God who walks alongside us, who gets involved in our lives, in our homes, in the midst of our "pots and pans," as Saint Teresa of Jesus liked to say.

MSG

ALL THE love God has in himself, all the beauty God has in himself, all the truth God has in himself, he entrusts to the family. A family is truly a family when it is capable of opening its arms to receive all that love. . . . [T]he garden of Eden is long gone; life has its problems; men and women—through the wiles of the devil—experienced division. And all that love God gave us was practically lost. And in no time, the first crime was committed, the first fratricide. Brother kills brother: war. God's love, beauty, and truth, and on the other hand the destructiveness of war: we are poised between those two realities even today. It is up to us to choose, to decide which way to go.

PVF

GOD CAME into the world in a family. And he could do this because that family was a family with a heart open to love, a family whose doors were open. We can think of Mary, a young woman. She can't believe it: "How can this be?" But once it was explained to her, she obeys. We think of Joseph, full of dreams for making a home; then along comes this surprise that he doesn't understand. He accepts; he obeys. And in the loving obedience of this woman, Mary, and this man, Joseph, we have a family into which God comes. God always knocks on the doors of our hearts. He likes to do that. He goes out from within. But do you know what he likes best of all? To knock on the doors of families. And to see families that are united; families that love; families that bring up their children, educating them and helping them to grow; families that build a society of goodness, truth, and beauty.

PVF

THE FAMILY has a divine identity card. Do you see what I mean? God gave the family an identity card, so that families could be places in our world where his truth, love, and beauty could continue to take root and grow. Some of you may say to me: "Father, you can say that because you're not married!" Certainly, in the family there are difficulties. In families we argue. . . . Families always, always, have crosses. Always. Because the love of God, the Son of God, also asked us to follow him along this way. But in families also, the cross is followed by resurrection, because there too the Son of God leads us. So the family is—if you excuse the word—a workshop of hope, of the hope of life and resurrection, since God was the one who opened this path.

PVF

THEN, TOO, there are children. Children are hard work. When we were children, we were hard work. Sometimes back home I see some of my staff who come to work with rings under their eyes. They have a one- or two-month-old baby.

And I ask them: "Didn't you get any sleep?" And they say: "No, the baby cried all night." In families, there are difficulties, but those difficulties are resolved by love. Hatred doesn't resolve any difficulty. Divided hearts do not resolve difficulties. Only love is capable of resolving difficulty. Love is a celebration; love is joy; love is perseverance.

PVF

WE HAVE to care in a special way for children and for grandparents. Children and young people are the future; they are our strength; they are what keep us moving forward. They are the ones in whom we put our hope. Grandparents are a family's memory. They are the ones who gave us the faith; they passed the faith on to us. Taking care of grandparents and taking care of children is the sign of love—I'm not sure if it is the greatest, but for the family I would say that it is the most promising—because it promises the future. A people incapable of caring for children and caring for the elderly is a people without a future, because it lacks the strength and the memory needed to move forward.

PVF

THE FAMILY is beautiful, but it takes hard work; it brings problems. In the family, sometimes there is fighting. The husband argues with the wife; they get upset with each other, or children get upset with their parents. May I offer a bit of advice? Never end the day without making peace in the family. In the family the day cannot end in fighting. May God bless you. May God give you strength. May God inspire you to keep moving forward. Let us care for the family. Let us defend the family, because there our future is at stake.

PVF

HOW IMPORTANT it is for us to share our home life and to help one another in this marvelous and challenging task of "being a family."

PVF

FROM TIME immemorial, in the depths of our heart, we have heard those powerful words: it is not good for you to be alone. The family is the great blessing, the great gift of this "God with us," who did not want to abandon us to the solitude of a life without others, without challenges, without a home.

PVF

GOD DOES not dream by himself, he tries to do everything "with us." His dream constantly comes true in the dreams of many couples who work to make their lives that of a family.

PVF

THAT IS why the family is the living symbol of the loving plan of which the Father once dreamed. To want to form a family is to resolve to be a part of God's dream, to choose to dream with him, to want to build with him, to join him in this saga of building a world where no one will feel alone, unwanted, or homeless.

PVF

LAYING DOWN one's life out of love is not easy. As with the Master, "staking everything" can sometimes involve the cross. [There are] times when everything seems uphill. I think of all those parents, all those families who lack employment or workers' rights, and how this is a true cross. How many sacrifices they make to earn their daily bread! It is understandable that, when these parents return home, they are so weary that they cannot give their best to their children.

PVF

WE CANNOT call any society healthy when it does not leave real room for family life. We cannot think that a society has a future when it fails to pass laws capable of protecting families and ensuring their basic needs, especially those of families just starting out. How many problems would be solved if our societies protected families and provided households—especially those of recently married couples—with the possibility of dignified work, housing, and healthcare services to accompany them throughout life.

PVF

LET US help one another to make it possible to "stake everything on love." Let us help one another at times of difficulty and lighten each other's burdens. Let us support one another. Let us be families that are a support for other families.

PVF

PERFECT FAMILIES do not exist. This must not discourage us. Quite the opposite. Love is something we learn; love is something we live; love grows as it is "forged" by the concrete situations that each particular family experiences. Love is born and constantly develops amid lights and shadows. Love can flourish in men and women who try not to make conflict the last word, but rather a new opportunity—an opportunity to seek help, an opportunity to question how we need to improve, an opportunity to discover the God who is with us and never abandons us. This is a great legacy that we can give to our children, a very good lesson: we make mistakes, yes; we have problems, yes. But we know that is not really what counts. We know that mistakes, problems, and conflicts are an opportunity to draw closer to others, to draw closer to God.

PVF

FOR THE Church, the family is not first and foremost a cause for concern, but rather the joyous confirmation of God's blessing upon the masterpiece of creation. Every day, all over the world, the Church can rejoice in the Lord's gift of so many families who, even amid difficult trials, remain faithful to their promises and keep the faith!

MBP

WE WOULD be mistaken, however, to see this "culture" of the present world as mere indifference toward marriage and the family, as pure and simple selfishness. Are today's young people hopelessly timid, weak, and inconsistent? We must not fall into this trap. Many young people, in the context of this culture of discouragement, have yielded to a form of unconscious acquiescence. They are afraid—deep down—paralyzed before the beautiful, noble, and truly necessary challenges. Many put off marriage while waiting for ideal conditions, when everything can be perfect. Meanwhile, life goes on, without really being lived to the full. For knowledge of life's true pleasures only comes as the fruit of a long-term, generous investment of our intelligence, enthusiasm, and passion.

MBP

WE NEED to invest our energies not so much in rehearsing the problems of the world around us and the merits of Christianity, but in extending a sincere invitation to young people to be brave and to opt for marriage and the family. In Buenos Aires, many women used to complain about their children who were 30, 32, or 34 years old and still single: "I don't know what to do." —"Well, stop ironing their shirts!" Young people have to be encouraged to take this risk, but it is a risk of fruitfulness and life.

MBP

WE CHRISTIANS, the Lord's disciples, ask the families of the world to help us! How many of us are here at this celebration! This is itself something prophetic, a kind of miracle in today's world, which is tired of inventing new divisions, new hurts, new disasters. Would that we could all be prophets! Would that all of us could be open to miracles of love to benefit our own families and all the families of the world, and thus overcome the scandal of a narrow, petty love, closed in on itself, impatient of others! I leave you with a question for each of you to answer—because I said the word "impatient": at home do we shout at one another or do we speak with love and tenderness? This is a good way of measuring our love.

MWM

AND HOW beautiful it would be if everywhere, even beyond our borders, we could appreciate and encourage this prophecy and this miracle! We renew our faith in the word of the Lord, which invites faithful families to this openness. It invites all those who want to share the prophecy of the covenant of man and woman, which generates life and reveals God! May the Lord help us to be sharers in the prophecy of peace, of tenderness and affection in the family. May his word help us to share in the prophetic sign of watching over our children and our grandparents with tenderness, with patience, and with love.

MWM

ANYONE WHO wants to bring into this world a family that teaches children to be excited by every gesture aimed at overcoming evil—a family that shows that the Spirit is alive and at work—will encounter our gratitude and our appreciation. Whatever the family, people, religion, or region to which they belong!

MWM

IT IS beautiful to have dreams and to be able to fight for our dreams. Don't ever forget this.

OLQ

HERE I see you smiling. Keep smiling and help bring joy to everyone you meet. It isn't always easy. Every home has its problems, difficult situations, sickness, but never stop dreaming so you can be happy.

OLQ

WHEREVER THERE are dreams, wherever there is joy, Jesus is always present. Always. But who is it that sows sadness, that sows mistrust, envy, evil desires? What is his name? The devil. The devil always sows sadness, because he doesn't want us to be happy; he doesn't want us to dream. Wherever there is joy, Jesus is always present because Jesus is joy, and he wants to help us to feel that joy every day of our lives.

OLQ

THE GOOD thing is that we also make new friends. This is very important, the new friends we make. We meet people who open doors for us, who are kind to us. They offer us friendship and understanding, and they try to help us not to feel like strangers, foreigners. People work hard to help us feel at home. Even if we sometimes think back on where we came from, we meet good people who help us feel at home. How nice it is to feel that our school or the places where we gather are a second home.

OLQ

PLEASE DON'T forget to pray for me, so that I can share with many people the joy of Jesus. And let us also pray that many other people can share joy like your own, whenever you feel supported, helped, and counseled. Even when there are problems, even then, we still feel peace in our hearts because Jesus never abandons us.

OLQ

Freedom:
A Precious
Possession

AMERICAN CATHOLICS are committed to building a society that is truly tolerant and inclusive, to safeguarding the rights of individuals and communities, and to rejecting every form of unjust discrimination. With countless other people of good will, they are likewise concerned that efforts to build a just and wisely ordered society respect their deepest concerns and their right to religious liberty. That freedom remains one of America's most precious possessions.

WCW

BUILDING A future of freedom requires love of the common good and cooperation in a spirit of subsidiarity and solidarity.

USC

IT IS important that today, as in the past, the voice of faith continues to be heard, for it is a voice of fraternity and love, which tries to bring out the best in each person and in each society. Such cooperation is a powerful resource in the battle to eliminate new global forms of slavery, born of grave injustices that can be overcome only through new policies and new forms of social consensus.

USC

THE DECLARATION of Independence stated that all men and women are created equal, that they are endowed by their Creator with certain inalienable rights, and that governments exist to protect and defend those rights. Those ringing words continue to inspire us today, even as they have inspired peoples throughout the world to

fight for the freedom to live in accordance with
their dignity.

IMP

HISTORY ALSO shows that these or any truths
must constantly be reaffirmed, re-appropriated,
and defended. The history of this nation is also
the tale of a constant effort, lasting to our own
day, to embody those lofty principles in social
and political life. We remember the great struggles that led to the abolition of slavery, the exten-
sion of voting rights, the growth of the labor
movement, and the gradual effort to eliminate
every kind of racism and prejudice directed at
further waves of new Americans.

IMP

ALL OF us benefit from remembering our past. A people that remembers does not repeat past errors; instead, it looks with confidence to the challenges of the present and the future. Remembrance saves a people's soul from whatever or whoever would attempt to dominate it or to use it for their own interests.

IMP

I WOULD like to reflect with you on the right to religious freedom. It is a fundamental right that shapes the way we interact socially and personally with our neighbors whose religious views differ from our own. The ideal of interreligious dialogue, where all men and women from different religious traditions can speak to one another without arguing, this is what religious freedom allows.

IMP

Religious freedom certainly means the right to worship God, individually and in community, as our consciences dictate. But religious liberty, by its nature, transcends places of worship and the private sphere of individuals and families. Because religion itself, the religious dimension, is not a subculture; it is part of the culture of every people and every nation.

IMP

OUR VARIOUS religious traditions serve society primarily by the message they proclaim. They call individuals and communities to worship God, the source of all life, liberty, and happiness. They remind us of the transcendent dimension of human existence and our irreducible freedom in the face of any claim to absolute power.

IMP

IN A world where various forms of modern tyranny seek to suppress religious freedom, or, as I said earlier, to try to reduce it to a subculture without right to a voice in the public square, or to use religion as a pretext for hatred and brutality, it is imperative that the followers of the various religious traditions join their voices in calling for peace, tolerance, and respect for the dignity and the rights of others.

IMP

LET US preserve freedom. Let us cherish freedom. Freedom of conscience, religious freedom, the freedom of each person, each family, each people, which is what gives rise to rights. May this country and each of you be renewed in gratitude for the many blessings and freedoms that you enjoy. And may you defend these rights, especially your religious freedom, for it has been given to you by God himself.

IMP

The Father's Merciful Embrace

WE ARE gathered here in Philadelphia to celebrate God's gift of family life. Within our family of faith and our human families, the sins and crimes of sexual abuse of children must no longer be held in secret and in shame. As we anticipate the Jubilee Year of Mercy, your presence, so generously given despite the anger and pain you have experienced, reveals the merciful heart of Christ. Your stories of survival, each unique and compelling, are powerful signs of the hope that comes from the Lord's promise to be with us always.

VSA

PRAY THAT many people of the Church will respond to the call to accompany those who have suffered abuse. May the Door of Mercy be opened wide in our dioceses, our parishes, our homes and our hearts, to receive those who were abused and to seek the path to forgiveness by trusting in the Lord. We promise to support your continued healing and to always be vigilant to protect the children of today and tomorrow.

VSA

WHEN THE disciples who walked with Jesus on the road to Emmaus recognized that he was the Risen Lord, they asked Jesus to stay with them. Like those disciples, I humbly beg you and all survivors of abuse to stay with us, to stay with the Church, and that together, as pilgrims on the journey of faith, we might find our way to the Father.

VSA

I FEEL many different emotions standing here at Ground Zero, where thousands of lives were taken in a senseless act of destruction. Here, grief is palpable. The water we see flowing toward that empty pit reminds us of all those lives that fell prey to those who think that destruction, tearing down, is the only way to settle conflicts. It is the silent cry of those who were victims of a mindset that knows only violence, hatred, and revenge; a mindset that can only cause pain, suffering, destruction, and tears.

GZM

THE FLOWING water is also a symbol of our tears. Tears at so much devastation and ruin, past and present. This is a place where we shed tears; we weep out of a sense of helplessness in the face of injustice, murder, and the failure to settle conflicts through dialogue. Here we mourn the wrongful and senseless loss of innocent lives because of the inability to find solutions that respect the common good. This flowing water reminds us of yesterday's tears, but also of all the tears still being shed today.

GZM

A FEW moments ago I met some of the families of the fallen first responders. Meeting them made me see once again how acts of destruction are never impersonal, abstract, or merely material. They always have a face, a concrete story, and names. In those family members, we see the face of pain, a pain that still touches us and cries out to heaven.

GZM

AMID PAIN and grief, we also have a palpable sense of the heroic goodness people are capable of, those hidden reserves of strength from which we can draw.

GZM

Commitment to
Peace and Justice

LET US implore from on high the gift of commitment to the cause of peace. Peace in our homes, our families, our schools, and our communities. Peace in all those places where war never seems to end. Peace for those faces that have known nothing but pain. Peace throughout this world that God has given us as the home of all and a home for all. Simply *peace*.

GZM

GOD OF peace, bring your peace to our
    violent world:
peace in the hearts of all men and women
and peace among the nations of the earth.
Turn to your way of love
those whose hearts and minds
are consumed with hatred,

and who justify killing in the name of religion.

GZM

OUR RICH religious traditions seek to offer meaning and direction, "they have an enduring power to open new horizons, to stimulate thought, to expand the mind and heart" (*Joy of the Gospel*, no. 256). They call to conversion, reconciliation, concern for the future of society, self-sacrifice in the service of the common good, and compassion for those in need. At the heart of their spiritual mission is the proclamation of the truth and dignity of the human person and all human rights.

IMP

THE WORLD seems to have become one of these great supermarkets; our culture has become more and more competitive. Business is no longer conducted on the basis of trust; others can no longer be trusted. There are no longer close personal relationships. Today's culture seems to encourage people not to bond with anything or anyone, not to trust. The most important thing nowadays seems to be to follow the latest trend or activity. This is even true of religion. Today consumption seems to determine what is important— consuming relationships, consuming friendships, consuming religions, consuming, consuming . . . whatever the cost or consequences. It's a kind of consumption that does not favor bonding, a consumption that has little to do with human relationships. Social bonds are a mere "means" for the satisfaction of "my needs." The important thing is no longer our neighbor, with his or her familiar face, story, and personality.

MBP

The Sacredness
of Human Life
and of Creation

THE INNOCENT victims of abortion; children who die of hunger or from bombings; immigrants who drown in the search for a better tomorrow; the elderly or the sick who are considered a burden; the victims of terrorism, wars, violence, and drug trafficking; the environment devastated by man's predatory relationship with nature—at stake in all of this is the gift of God, of which we are noble stewards but not masters. It is wrong, then, to look the other way or to remain silent.

MBW

IT IS my wish that throughout my visit the family should be a recurrent theme. How essential the family has been to building this country! And how worthy it remains of our support and encouragement! Yet I cannot hide my concern for the family, which is threatened, perhaps as never before, from within and without. Fundamental relationships are being called into question, as is the very basis of marriage and the family. I can only reiterate the importance and, above all, the richness and the beauty of family life.

USC

THIS CONVICTION has led me, from the beginning of my ministry, to advocate at different levels for the global abolition of the death penalty. I am convinced that this way is the best, since every life is sacred, every human person is endowed with an inalienable dignity, and society can only benefit from the rehabilitation of those convicted of crimes.

USC

AT THE same time, government leaders must do everything possible to ensure that all can have the minimum spiritual and material means needed to live in dignity and to create and support a family, which is the primary cell of any social development. In practical terms, this absolute minimum has three names: lodging, labor, and land; and one spiritual name: spiritual freedom, which includes religious freedom, the right to education, and all other civil rights.

UNO

THIS PLACE of death [Twin Towers] became a place of life too, a place of saved lives, a hymn to the triumph of life over the prophets of destruction and death, to goodness over evil, to reconciliation and unity over hatred and division.

GZM

EVERY CREATURE, particularly a living creature, has an intrinsic value, in its existence, its life, its beauty, and its interdependence with other creatures. We Christians, together with the other monotheistic religions, believe that the universe is the fruit of a loving decision by the Creator, who permits man respectfully to use creation for the good of his fellow men and for the glory of the Creator; he is not authorized to abuse it, much less to destroy it. In all religions, the environment is a fundamental good (cf. *Laudato Si'*, no. 81).

UNO

THE MISUSE and destruction of the environment are also accompanied by a relentless process of exclusion. In effect, a selfish and boundless thirst for power and material prosperity leads both to the misuse of available natural resources and to the exclusion of the weak and disadvantaged, either because they are differently abled (handicapped), or because they lack adequate information and technical expertise, or are incapable of decisive political action. Economic and social exclusion is a complete denial of human fraternity and a grave offense against human rights and the environment. The poorest are those who suffer most from such offenses, for three serious reasons: they are cast off by society, forced to live off what is discarded, and suffer unjustly from the abuse of the environment. They are part of today's widespread and quietly growing "culture of waste."

UNO

CREATION IS compromised "where we ourselves have the final word. . . . The misuse of creation begins when we no longer recognize any instance above ourselves, when we see nothing else but ourselves" (*Address to the Clergy of the Diocese of Bolzano-Bressanone*, August 6, 2008). Consequently, the defense of the environment and the fight against exclusion demand that we recognize a moral law written into human nature itself, one that includes the natural difference between man and woman (cf. *Laudato Si'*, no. 155), and absolute respect for life in all its stages and dimensions (cf. ibid., nos. 123, 136).

UNO

THE COMMON home of all men and women must continue to rise on the foundations of a right understanding of universal fraternity and respect for the sacredness of every human life, of every man and every woman, the poor, the elderly, children, the infirm, the unborn, the unemployed, the abandoned, those considered disposable because they are only considered as part of a statistic. This common home of all men and women must also be built on the understanding of a certain sacredness of created nature.

UNO

BEAUTY BRINGS us to God. And a truthful witness brings us to God, because God is also truth. He is beauty, and he is truth. A witness intended to help others is good; it makes us good, because God is goodness. It brings us to God. All that is good, all that is true, and all that is beautiful brings us to God. Because God is good; God is beauty; God is truth.

PVF

GOD CREATED the world. God made this wonderful world in which we live. . . . But the most beautiful thing God made—so the Bible tells us—was the family. He created man and woman.

And he gave them everything. He entrusted the world to them: "Grow, multiply, cultivate the earth, make it bear fruit, let it grow." All the love he put into that marvelous creation, he entrusted to a family.

PVF

God in the City

WE HAVE listened to the words: *"The people who walked in darkness have seen a great light"* (Is 9:1).

The people who walked—caught up in their activities and routines, amid their successes and failures, their worries and expectations—have seen a great light. The people who walked—with all their joys and hopes, their disappointments and regrets—have seen a great light.

MSG

IN EVERY age, the People of God are called to contemplate this light. A light for the nations, as the elderly Simeon joyfully expressed it. A light meant to shine on every corner of this city, on our fellow citizens, on every part of our lives.

MSG

"THE PEOPLE who walked in darkness have seen a great light." One special quality of God's people is their ability to see, to contemplate, even in "moments of darkness," the light that Christ brings. God's faithful people can see, discern, and contemplate his living presence in the midst of life, in the midst of the city. Together with the prophet Isaiah, we can say: The people who walk, breathe, and live in the midst of smog have seen a great light, have experienced a breath of fresh air.

MSG

LIVING IN a big city is not always easy. A multicultural context presents many complex challenges. Yet big cities are a reminder of the hidden riches present in our world: in the diversity of its cultures, traditions, and historical experiences; in

the variety of its languages, costumes, and cuisine.
Big cities bring together all the different ways that
we human beings have discovered to express the
meaning of life, wherever we may be.

MSG

KNOWING THAT Jesus still walks our streets,
that he is part of the lives of his people, that he is
involved with us in one vast history of salvation,
fills us with hope: a hope that liberates us from
the forces pushing us to isolation and lack of
concern for the lives of others, for the life of our
city; a hope that frees us from empty "connec-
tions," from abstract analyses, or sensationalist
routines; a hope that is unafraid of involvement,
that acts as a leaven wherever we happen to live
and work; a hope that makes us see, even in the

midst of smog, the presence of God as he continues to walk the streets of our city. Because God is in the city.

MSG

WHAT IS it like, this light traveling through our streets? How do we encounter God, who lives with us amid the smog of our cities? How do we encounter Jesus, alive and at work in the daily life of our multicultural cities?

MSG

GO OUT to others and share the good news that God, our Father, walks at our side. He frees us from anonymity, from a life of emptiness, and brings us to the school of encounter. He removes us from the fray of competition and self-absorption, and he opens before us the path of peace—that peace which is born of accepting others, that peace which fills our hearts whenever we look upon those in need as our brothers and sisters.

MSG

GOD IS living in our cities. The Church is living in our cities. God and the Church living in our cities want to be like yeast in the dough, to relate to everyone, to stand at everyone's side . . .

MSG

Go Out and
Proclaim This Joy

WE ARE promoters of the culture of encounter. We are living sacraments of the embrace between God's riches and our poverty. We are witnesses of the abasement and the condescension of God who anticipates in love our every response.

MBW

DIALOGUE IS our method, not as a shrewd strategy but out of fidelity to the One who never wearies of visiting the marketplace, even at the eleventh hour, to propose his offer of love (see Mt 20:1–16).

MBW

WE ALL know the anguish felt by the first Eleven, huddled together, assailed and overwhelmed by the fear of sheep scattered because the shepherd had been struck. But we also know that we have been given a spirit of courage and not of timidity. So we cannot let ourselves be paralyzed by fear.

MBW

WE NEED to let the Lord's words echo constantly in our hearts: *"Take my yoke upon you, and learn from me, who am meek and humble of heart, and you will find refreshment for your souls"* (Mt 11:28–30). Jesus' yoke is a yoke of love and thus a pledge of refreshment. At times in our work we can be burdened by a sense of loneliness, and so we feel the heaviness of the yoke that we forget we have received it from the Lord. It seems to be ours alone, and so we drag it like weary oxen working a dry field, troubled by the thought that we are laboring in vain. We can forget the profound refreshment that is indissolubly linked to the One who has made us the promise.

MBW

THIS KIND of witness is a beacon whose light can reassure men and women sailing through the dark clouds of life that a sure haven awaits them, that they will not crash on the reefs or be overwhelmed by the waves.

MBW

JESUS GIVES the answer. He said to his disciples then and he says it to us now: Go forth! Proclaim! The joy of the Gospel is something to be experienced, something to be known and lived only through giving it away, through giving ourselves away.

JSW

A CHRISTIAN finds joy in mission: Go out to people of every nation!

JSW

A CHRISTIAN finds ever new joy in answering a call: Go forth and anoint!

JSW

GO OUT and in my name embrace life as it is, and not as you think it should be. Go out to the highways and byways, go out to tell the good news fearlessly—without prejudice, without superiority, without condescension—to all those who have lost the joy of living.

JSW

GO OUT to proclaim the merciful embrace of the Father. Go out to those who are burdened by pain and failure, who feel that their lives are empty, and proclaim the folly of a loving Father who wants to anoint them with the oil of hope, the oil of salvation. Go out to proclaim the good news that error, deceitful illusions, and falsehoods do not have the last word in a person's life. Go out with the ointment that soothes wounds and heals hearts.

JSW

THE CHURCH, the holy People of God, treads the dust-laden paths of history, so often traversed by conflict, injustice, and violence, in order to encounter her children, our brothers and sisters. The holy and faithful People of God are not afraid of losing their way; they are afraid of becoming self-enclosed, frozen into elites, clinging to their own security. They know that self-enclosure, in all the forms it takes, is the cause of so much apathy.

JSW

FATHER SERRA had a motto that inspired his life and work, not just a saying, but above all a reality that shaped the way he lived: *siempre adelante!* Keep moving forward! For him, this was the way to continue experiencing the joy of the Gospel, to keep his heart from growing numb, from being anesthetized. He kept moving forward, because the Lord was waiting. He kept going, because his brothers and sisters were waiting. He kept going forward to the end of his life. Today, like him, may we be able to say: Forward! Let's keep moving forward!

JSW

THE GOSPELS tell us how many people came up to Jesus to ask: "Master, what must we do?" The first thing that Jesus does in response is to propose, to encourage, to motivate. He keeps telling his disciples to go, to go out. He urges them to go out and meet others where they really are, not where we think they should be. Go out, again and again, go out without fear, go out without hesitation. Go out and proclaim this joy that is for all the people.

MSG

MOST OF you know the story of Saint Katharine Drexel, one of the great saints raised up by this local Church. When she spoke to Pope Leo XIII of the needs of the missions, the Pope—he was a very wise Pope!—asked her pointedly: "What about you? What are you going to do?" Those words changed Katharine's life, because they reminded her that, in the end, every Christian man and woman, by virtue of Baptism, has received a mission. Each one of us has to respond, as best we can, to the Lord's call to build up his Body, the Church.

BCR

THOSE WORDS—"WHAT about you?"— were addressed to a young person, a young woman with high ideals, and they changed her life. They made her think of the immense work that had to be done, and to realize that she was being called to do her part. How many young people in our parishes and schools have the same high ideals, generosity of spirit, and love for Christ and the Church! I ask you: Do we challenge them? Do we make space for them and help them to do their part; to find ways of sharing their enthusiasm and gifts with our communities, above all in works of mercy and concern for others? Do we share our own joy and enthusiasm in serving the Lord?

BCR

THE CHURCH in the United States has always devoted immense effort to the work of catechesis and education. Our challenge today is to build on those solid foundations and to foster a sense of collaboration and shared responsibility in planning for the future of our parishes and institutions.

BCR

SHOULD WE blame our young people for having grown up in this kind of society? Should we condemn them for living in this kind of a world? Should they hear their pastors saying that "it was all better back then," "the world is falling apart and if things go on this way, who knows where we will end up?" . . . No, I do not think that this is the way. . . . [W]e are asked to seek out, to accompany, to lift up, to bind up the wounds of our time. . . . "It is vitally important for the Church today to go forth and preach the Gospel to all: to all places, on all occasions, without hesitation, reluctance, or fear. The joy of the Gospel is for all people: no one can be excluded" (*Joy of the Gospel*, no. 23). The Gospel is not a product to be consumed; it is not a part of this culture of consumption.

MBP

IF WE prove capable of the demanding task of reflecting God's love, cultivating infinite patience and serenity as we strive to sow its seeds in the frequently crooked furrows in which we are called to plant—for very often we really do have to sow in crooked furrows—then even a Samaritan woman with five "non-husbands" will discover that she is capable of giving witness. And for every rich young man who with sadness feels that he has to calmly keep considering the matter, an older publican will come down from the tree and give fourfold to the poor, to whom, before that moment, he had never even given a thought.

MBP

Index of Talks

Pauline
BOOKS & MEDIA

A mission of the Daughters of St. Paul

As apostles of Jesus Christ, evangelizing
today's world:

We are CALLED to holiness
by God's living Word and Eucharist.

We COMMUNICATE the Gospel message
through our lives and through all
available forms of media.

We SERVE the Church
by responding to the hopes and needs
of all people with the Word of God,
in the spirit of St. Paul.

For more information visit our Web site:
www.pauline.org.

BOOKS & MEDIA

The Daughters of St. Paul operate book and media centers at the following addresses. Visit, call, or write the one nearest you today, or find us at www.pauline.org.

CALIFORNIA
3908 Sepulveda Blvd, Culver City, CA 90230   310-397-8676
935 Brewster Avenue, Redwood City, CA 94063   650-369-4230
5945 Balboa Avenue, San Diego, CA 92111   858-565-9181

FLORIDA
145 S.W. 107th Avenue, Miami, FL 33174   305-559-6715

HAWAII
1143 Bishop Street, Honolulu, HI 96813   808-521-2731

ILLINOIS
172 North Michigan Avenue, Chicago, IL 60601   312-346-4228

LOUISIANA
4403 Veterans Memorial Blvd, Metairie, LA 70006 504-887-7631

MASSACHUSETTS
885 Providence Hwy, Dedham, MA 02026   781-326-5385

MISSOURI
9804 Watson Road, St. Louis, MO 63126   314-965-3512

NEW YORK
64 West 38th Street, New York, NY 10018   212-754-1110

SOUTH CAROLINA
243 King Street, Charleston, SC 29401   843-577-0175

TEXAS
Currently no book center; for parish exhibits or outreach evangelization, contact: 210-569-0500, or SanAntonio@paulinemedia.com, or P.O. Box 761416, San Antonio, TX 78245

VIRGINIA
1025 King Street, Alexandria, VA 22314   703-549-3806

CANADA
3022 Dufferin Street, Toronto, ON M6B 3T5   416-781-9131

¡También somos su fuente para libros,
videos y música en español!